# EXPLORING VIOLIN HOLIDAY
## LEVEL 1A
### BY CHRISTINE SAVIDGE

Book Cover and Character Design by
*Burn Bright Creative Company*
Other Artwork: Adobe Stock

ExploringStrings.com

## Special Thanks

This project would not have been possible without the support and contributions of many wonderful people. To my family and friends — thank you for standing by me every step of the way. A special thanks to Alyssa for her vast knowledge of educational materials, and to Yoonhae and Lindsay for proofreading. Lindsay, thank you for your wisdom and for introducing me to Nate. To my teachers — Jillian Chrisman, Vladimir Krakovich, and Anna Vayman — thank you for setting examples of what it means to be a great teacher and for never giving up on me. And to my students — thank you for teaching me the lessons that can't be found in textbooks, and for playtesting the books with such enthusiasm. I am deeply grateful to you all!

## About The Author

Christine Savidge is a violinist and educator with 20-plus years of experience teaching violin, viola, and piano. She studied Music Education and Violin Performance at Ball State University, where she cultivated her passion for helping students become confident, skilled musicians. Her teaching is shaped by her training with both Suzuki and traditional violin teachers, allowing her to draw from a wide range of pedagogical styles. As part of a long tradition of teachers dedicated to strong technique and musicality, she created Exploring Strings. This vibrant string method is both engaging and visually appealing, while incorporating music theory, history, and other relevant content. When she is not teaching or performing in local symphonies, Christine enjoys gardening, dancing, and going on new adventures with friends.

ISBN: 979-8-9993244-2-9

First edition 2025

# Contents

**Note Reference Guide**

# Canon in D

Johann Pachelbel

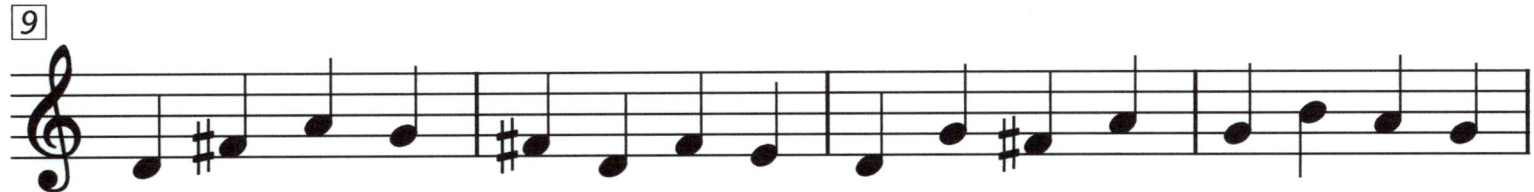

# Frog Went Courtin'

Traditional

Frog went courtin' and he did ride, uh huh
Rode up to Miss Mous–ie's door, uh huh.

Frog went courtin' and he did ride, uh huh.
Rode up to Miss Mous–ie's door, uh huh.

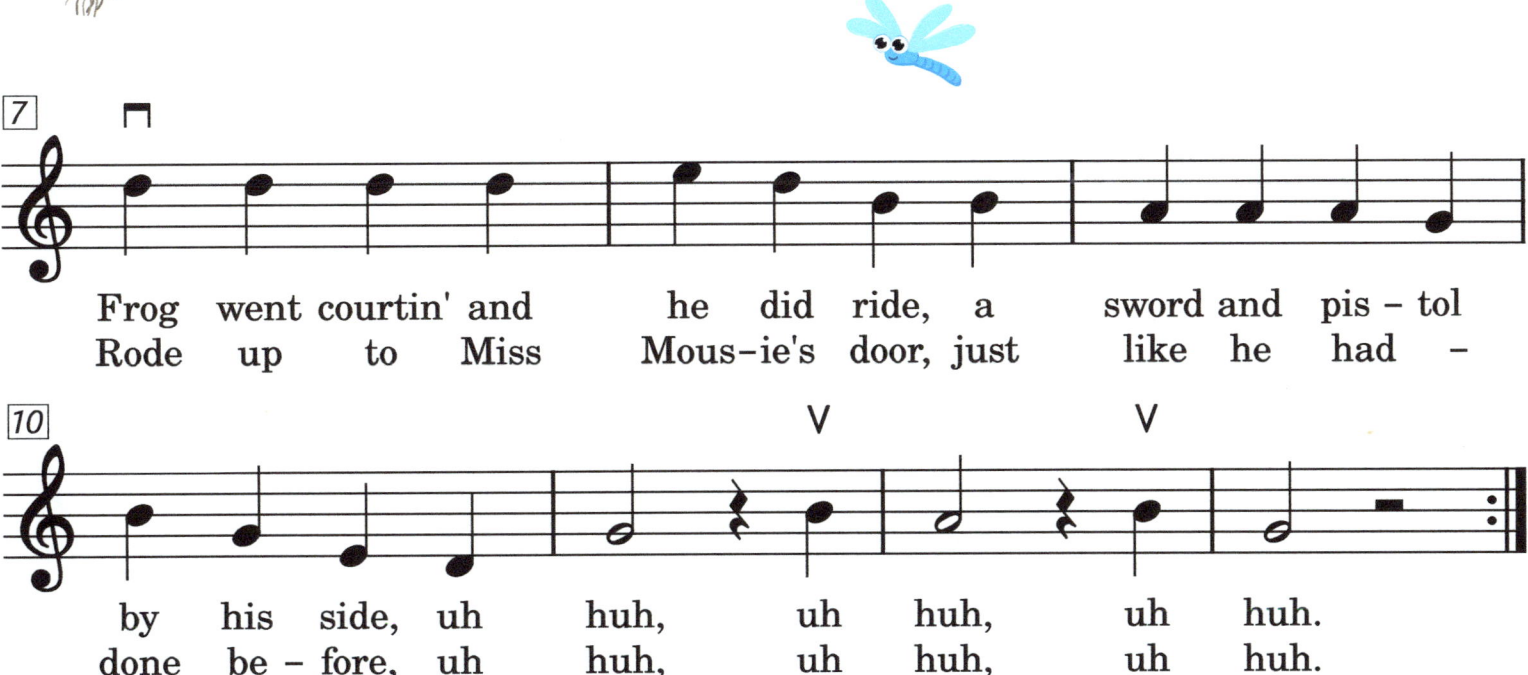

Frog went courtin' and he did ride, a sword and pis – tol
Rode up to Miss Mous-ie's door, just like he had –

by his side, uh huh, uh huh, uh huh.
done be – fore, uh huh, uh huh, uh huh.

# Easter

# Hot Cross Buns

Traditional

Hot   cross   buns!   Hot   cross   buns!

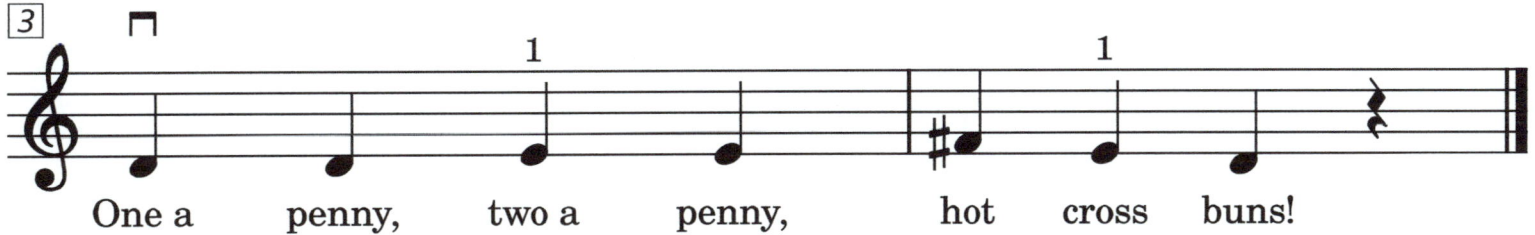

One a   penny,   two a   penny,   hot   cross   buns!

# Tis' Midnight And On Olive's Brow

Samuel Goldfarb

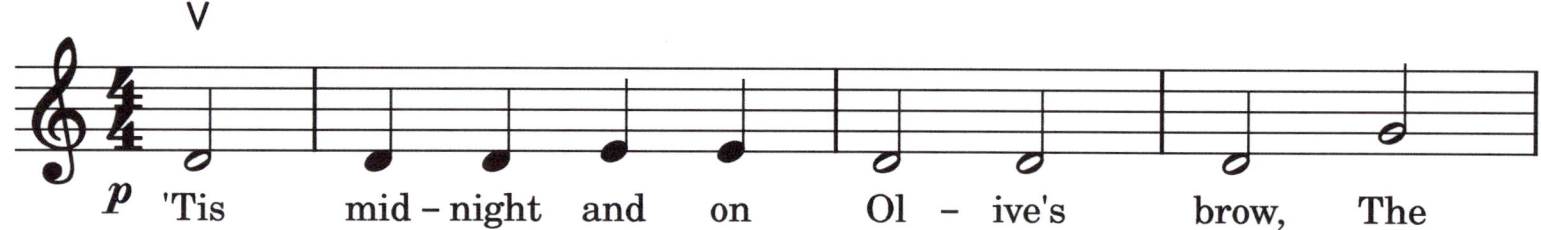

'Tis mid-night and on Ol – ive's brow, The

star is dimmed that late – ly shone: 'Tis mid-night in the

gar – den now, The suf-f'ring Sav – ior prays a – lone.

# Spooky Shadows

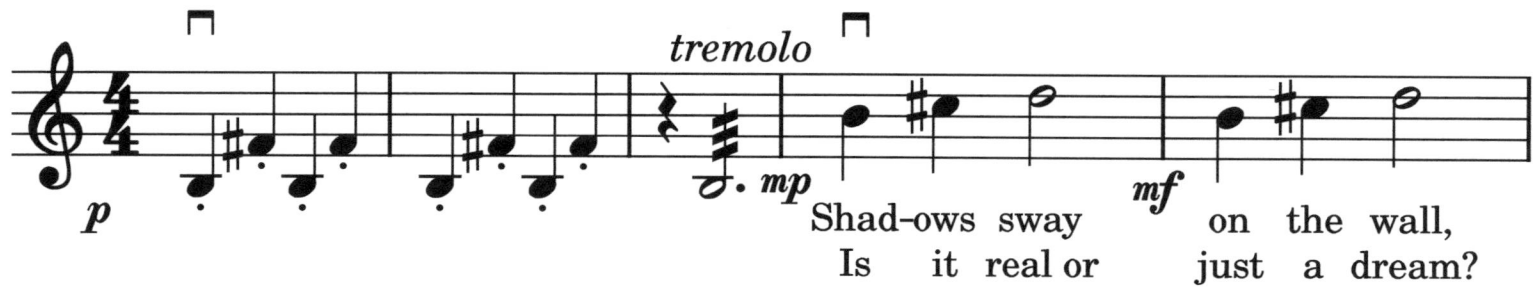

*tremolo*

*p*  *mp* Shad-ows sway   *mf* on the wall,
     Is   it real or       just a dream?

**Slide 2nd finger up and away.**

*f* big   and   tall,        in   the   hall   –
   Glow-ing   eyes.      Don't  you  scream

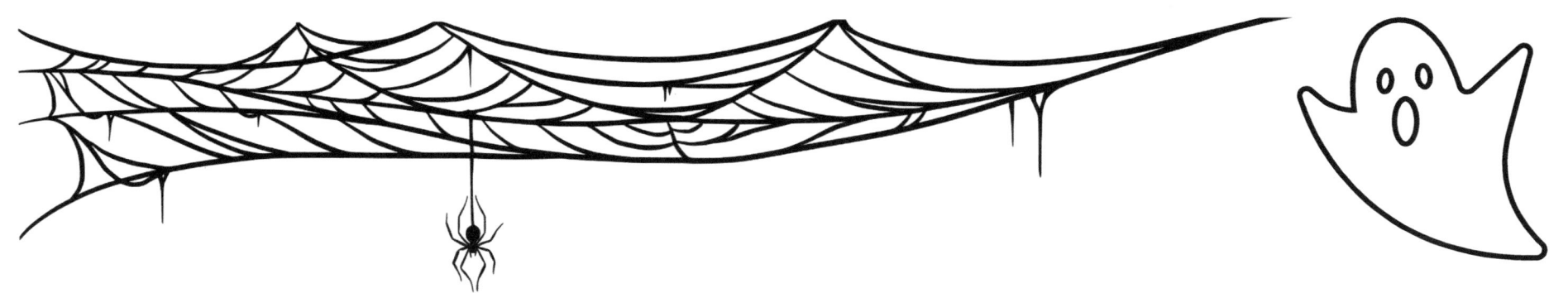

Boo boo boo they say to you. Spook-y night what will you do.

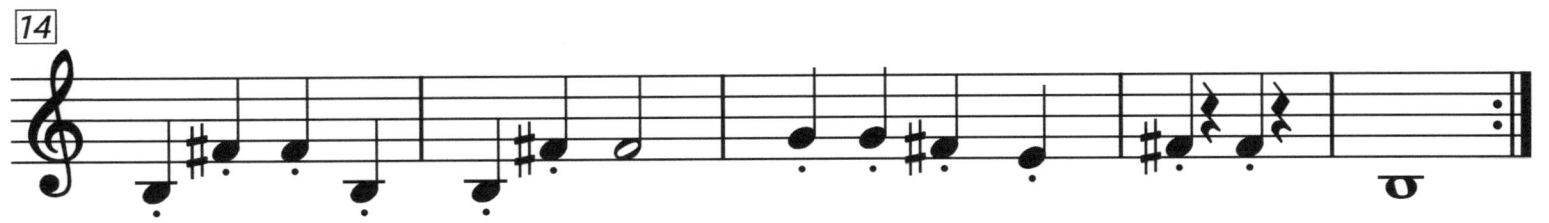

Boo boo boo its Hal-lo-ween, spook-i-est you've e-ver seen.

# The Bear

Vladimir Rebikov

Thanksgiving

# Jingle Bells

James Lord Pierpont

Jin – gle bells    jin – gle bells    jin – gle all the    way.

Oh what fun   it    is   to ride  a    one horse o – pen    sleigh.  hey!

9

Jin – gle bells    jin – gle bells    jin – gle all the way.

13

Oh what fun it    is to ride a    one horse o – pen sleigh!

# Autumn

Antonio Vivaldi

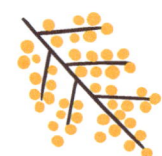

# Hanukkah

# Dreidel

Samuel and Israel Goldfarb

I have a lit-tle drei-del. I made it out of clay, and

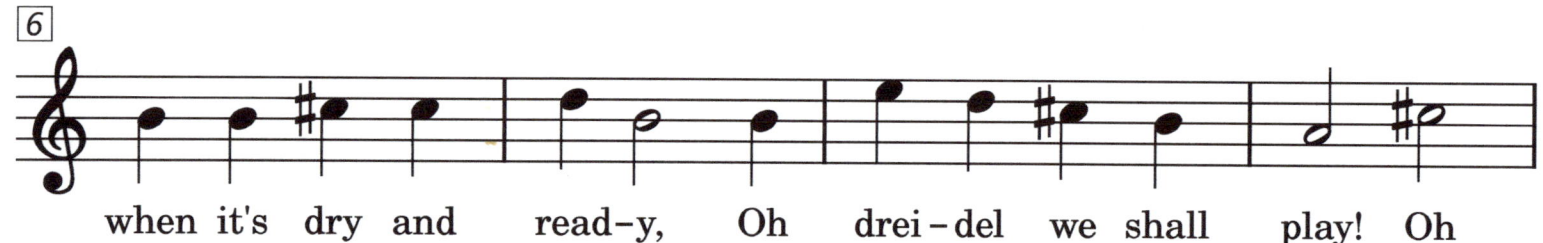

when it's dry and read-y, Oh drei-del we shall play! Oh

drei-del, drei-del, drei-del, I made you out of clay, and

when you're dry and read-y, Oh Drei-del we shall play.

CHRISTMAS

# Good King Wenceslas

P. Cantiones

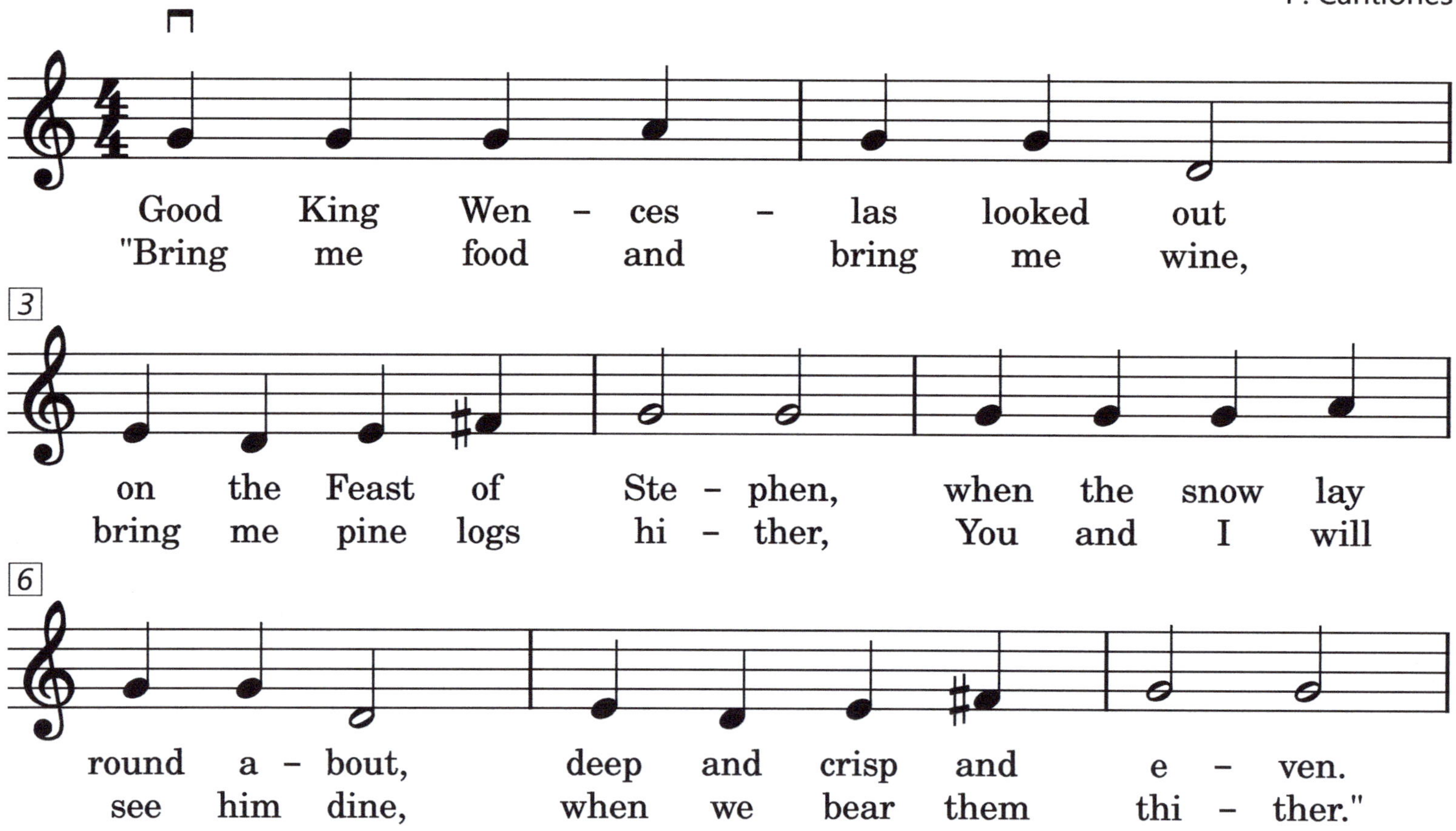

Good / "Bring   King / me   Wen / food   – ces / and   –   las / bring   looked / me   out / wine,

**3**   on / bring   the / me   Feast / pine   of / logs   Ste / hi – phen, / – ther,   when / You   the / and   snow / I   lay / will

**6**   round / see   a – bout, / him dine,   deep / when   and / we   crisp / bear   and / them   e / thi – ven. / – ther."

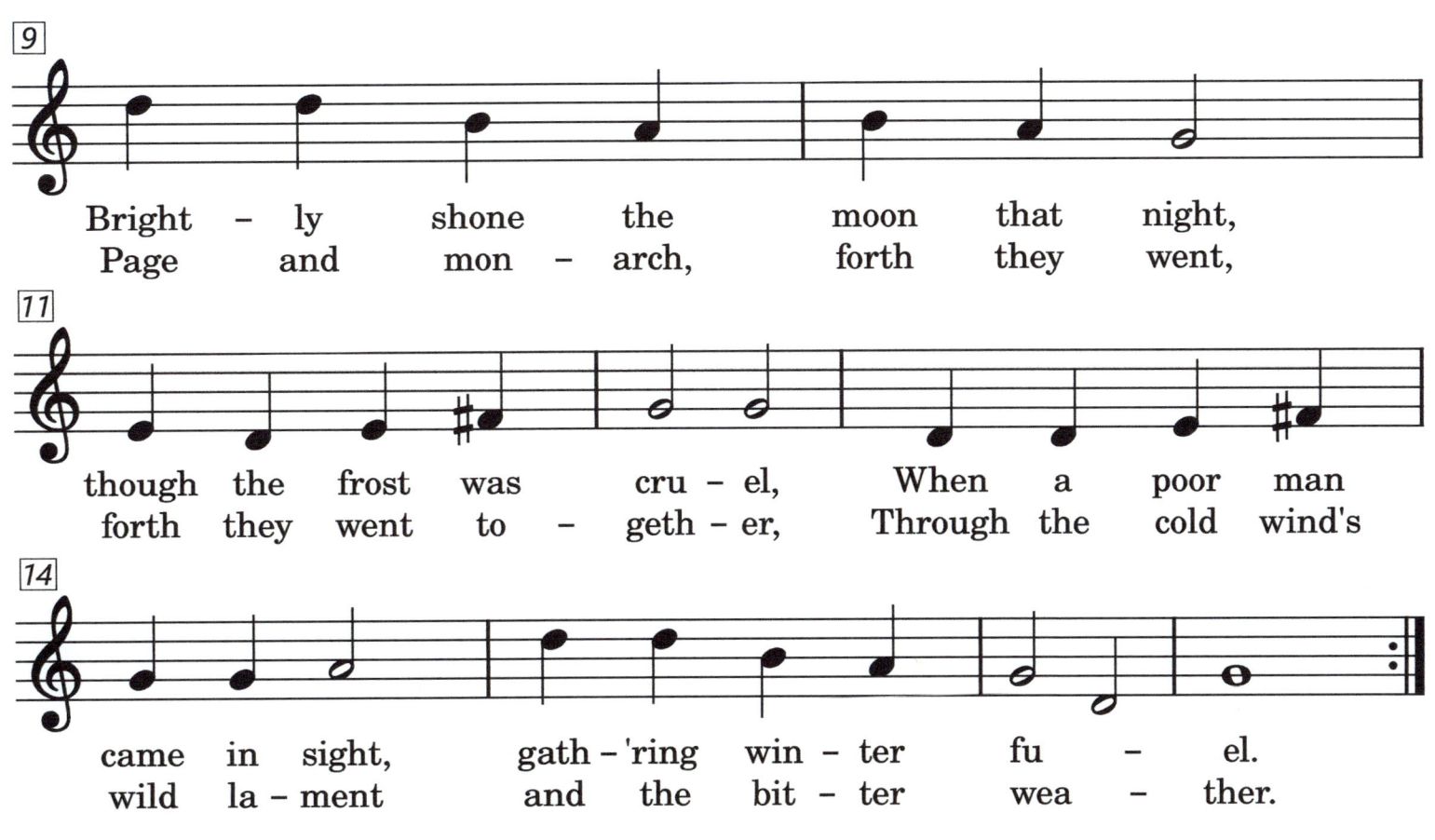

9

Bright – ly shone the moon that night,
Page and mon – arch, forth they went,

11

though the frost was cru – el, When a poor man
forth they went to – geth – er, Through the cold wind's

14

came in sight, gath –'ring win – ter fu – el.
wild la – ment and the bit – ter wea – ther.

# Jolly Old St. Nicholas

Traditional

*mf* Jol – ly Old St. Nich–o–las lean your ear this way!

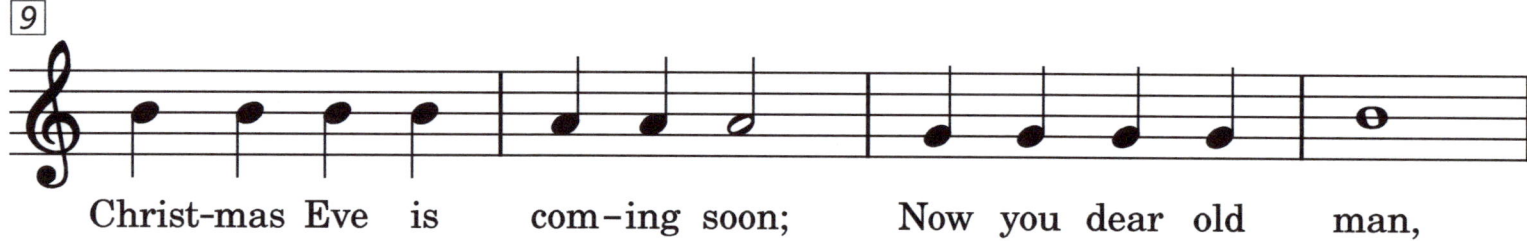

Don't you tell a sing–le soul, what I'm going to say;

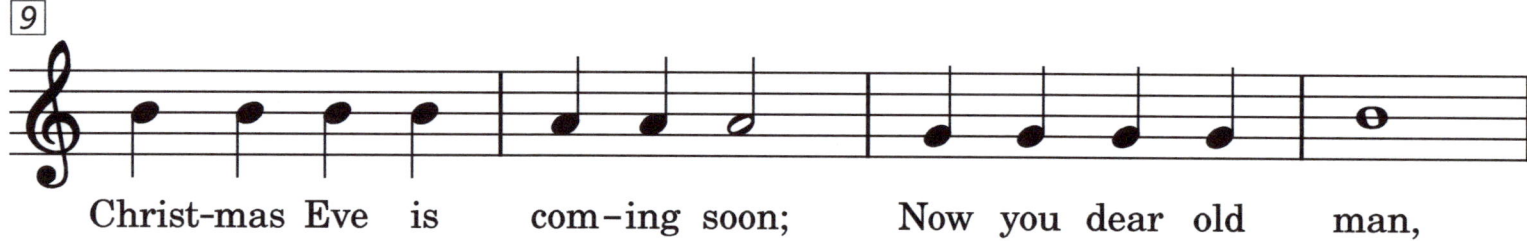

Christ–mas Eve is com–ing soon; Now you dear old man,

Whis–per what you'll bring to me, Tell me if you can.

New Year

# He's A Jolly Good Fellow

Traditional

*f* He's a jol – ly good fel – low. For he's a

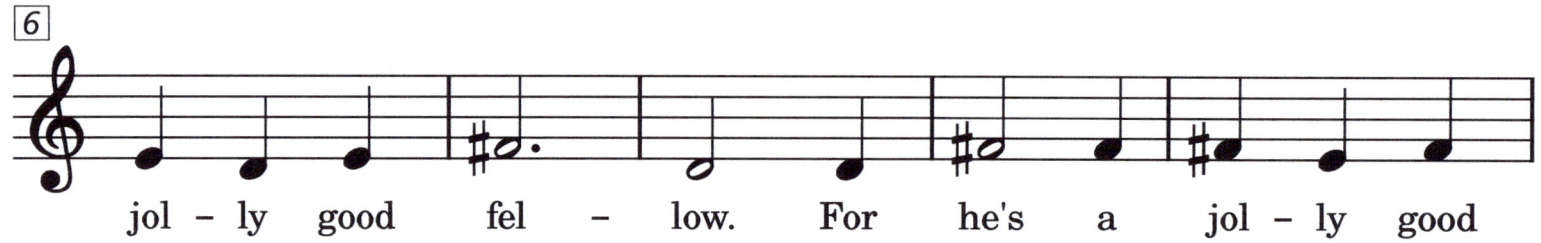

jol – ly good fel – low. For he's a jol – ly good

fel – low, and so say all of us!

# Note Reference Guide

All of the notes in this book can be found in the chart below.

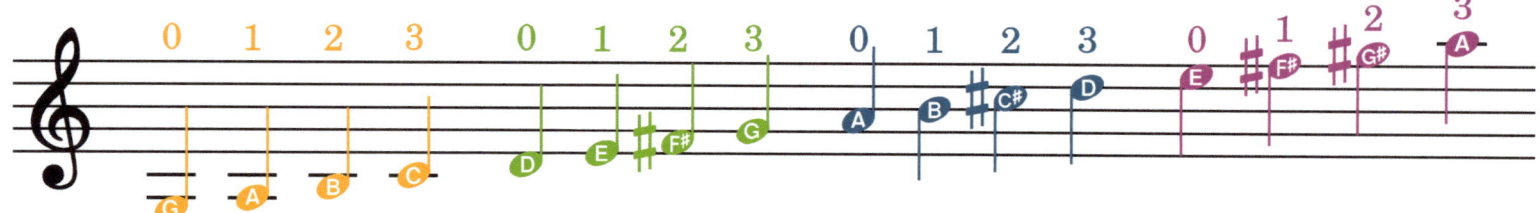

# Music Dictionary

**Quarter Note:** One beat.

**Half Note:** Two beats.

**Dotted Half Note:** Three beats.

**Whole Note:** Four beats.

**Quarter Rest:** One beat of silence.

**Half Rest:** Two beats of silence.

*p* **Piano:** Soft.

*mf* **Mezzo Forte:** Medium loud.

*f* **Forte:** Loud.

**Repeat Dots:** Play again.

**Staccato:** Detached. Shorten the note slightly and stop the bow.

**Tremolo:** Play in the upper part of the bow with small, quick movements. Keep arm relaxed.